It's the Cup! We can do it, lads!

Now Will can go for it.

He will score lots of goals!

It's a bad kick.
Will is mad.

It's a pen!

Will kicks a wicked ball!
He scores!

 He has won the Cup for the Cats

But it was the pads, not me!
But Will, I got you **new** pads!

New pads?
So was it the pads?
No, it was me!
I won the Cup!